Twenty-One Values
of Real Men & Boys

Other recent books by this author include

How to Quit Smoking in Only Three Days
Available on Amazon Kindle

The Seven Habits of Happily Retired People
Available hard copy or Amazon Kindle

Home Automation Made Easy
Hard copy or e-book

Build Your Own Free to Air Satellite TV System
Hard copy or e-book

The *Dennis the Mentor*™ Series:

Cover Your Six Leadership

DENNIS
the Mentor™

Twenty-One Values of Real Men & Boys

Defining manhood
in the twenty-first century
and beyond

Dennis C. Brewer

First Edition

© Dennis C. Brewer
Copper Cove Publishing
45170 US HWY 41
Chassell, Michigan 49916

Printed in the United States of America
April 15, 2015
Copper Cove Publishing, Chassell, Michigan

ISBN-13: 978-0-9795559-4-7
ISBN-10:   0-9795559-4-9

About the Author

Dennis C. Brewer was born in Michigan's Upper Peninsula and is a graduate of Michigan Technological University. He holds a Bachelor of Science degree in Business Administration. Dennis is a veteran of military service to the United States of America, which includes enlisted service in the Navy and commissioned officer service in the Army Reserve and Michigan's Army National Guard. His varied career paths included experiences in military, state, and federal government; private enterprise; and his own technology consulting practice. Travel to Japan, Taiwan, China, Hong Kong, England, Canada, Germany, and the Philippines contribute to Dennis's world view and humanitarian perspectives. Dennis has many nationally published books and magazine articles included in his writing credits.

Dennis C. Brewer began the importance of internalizing values at an early age. In Junior Army R.O.T.C training while in high school, he received many awards and medals over a four-year period. After high school, Dennis joined the Navy and quickly attained the rank of Chief Petty Officer (CPO) as one of the youngest CPOs in the Navy at that time. Like many of his highly motivated contemporaries, Dennis decided to become an officer and simultaneously joined the Michigan Army National Guard as an enlisted member and enrolled in Michigan Technological

University and the Senior Army R.O.T.C. program. Upon completion of his degree, Dennis was commissioned as a Second Lieutenant in the United States Army Reserve. After graduating with high academic honors from the Army Engineer Officer Basic Course at Fort Belvoir, VA, he returned to serve in the Michigan Army Guard, retiring as a Captain after assignments in many types of engineer units over twelve years, including recon officer, platoon leader, utilities engineer, and automation projects officer. One might say this immersion in courses, coaching, and experience where many organization core values were taught as operational principles qualify Captain Brewer with some degree of expertise on the topic of values, without taking into account his later remarkable careers in federal and state government, and in his own consulting practice.

Contents

About the Dennis the Mentor™ Series   xiii

Disclaimer   xvii

Foreword   xix

Prologue   1

Internal Values Do Drive Behavior   21

Value 1
Truth   25

Value 2
Learning   29

Value 3
Leadership   33

Value 4
Perseverance   37

Value 5
Diligence   39

Value 6
Faith   41

Contents

Value 7
Friendship   43

Value 8
Forgiveness   45

Value 9
Diversity   47

Value 10
Modesty   49

Value 11
Sensitivity   51

Value 12
Creativity   53

Value 13
Contribution   55

Value 14
Collaboration   57

Value 15
Encouragement   59

Value 16
Gratitude   61

Value 17
Respect   63

Value 18
Responsibility   67

Value 19
Restraint   69

Value 20
Risk   71

Value 21
Success   73

The Other 4 Percent:
Recognizing Men Void of Values   75

About the Dennis the Mentor™ Series

Ten points about this series and its name.

1. In the publisher's view, everyone should have helpful mentors who can offer sage advice at important
times on life's journey—all the way from a child's
first communication to the end of life's journey.

2. Unfortunately, sufficient quantities of sagacious
mentors are unavailable to everyone, so a book such
as this can help fill the void.

3. The readily available mentors and would-be-mentors
in any geographic area don't always offer the best
advice and counsel.

4. Dysfunctional families, single-parent families,
one-minute parenting practices, less-than-stellar
public and private educational institutions, and a
shortage of true moral champions across society all
lead to a shortage of suitable mentors.

5. The ideas, advice, and topical discussion in this series
are offered up as one of many potential inputs for
the reader to help them find their own solutions to
problems or issues.

6. The information in each book is to be treated as simple advice from an author who is interested in these topics and has thought about them deeply enough to be willing to share his opinions in a natural and organized format.

7. The series recognizes that its typical reader is a very intelligent individual with some expertise of their own. This reader also wants to learn additional information and other points of view on the topics presented.

8. The texts are intended to offer insights to also help readers who haven't had the exposure to the topics or the opportunity to experience the subject matter themselves.

9. Mentors can be, if nothing else, entertaining, and so can a little book like this.

10. Anything you read can lead to new perceptions about yourself and the universe, as well as the people and things in that universe.

I dedicate this book to all those children who are growing up without positive role models in their homes, families, or neighborhoods. It is also dedicated to individuals, families, and neighborhoods suffering from the consequences brought about by the actions of individuals and groups devoid of a dignified core-value system.

Disclaimer

This book is written with the idea in mind to provide information that may be of interest regarding the subject matter covered. It is sold with the understanding that the publisher and author are not engaged in rendering medical, nutritional, legal, accounting, or any other professional services for that matter. If medical, professional, or other subject matter expert advice is required, then the services of one or more competent professionals known as experts in the field relating to the subject matter should be sought for advice and counsel.

The purpose of this book is not to reprint all the information that is otherwise available to the author or publisher on this topic, but to complement, amplify, and/or supplement other available texts on the topics. You are encouraged to read all other material available, learn as much as possible about these topics and adapt the information to suit your individual needs.

You, not the author, are personally responsible for all your actions. The author accepts no liability for your success or failure to use the ideas in this book. Nor does the author accept any liability for any claims of harm or damage resulting from the use or misuse of any of the concepts or ideas in this book. The author accepts no liability

Disclaimer

from your seeking, or failure to seek, competent professional advice on the topics covered in this book or use of
the ideas in this book. This information is provided as an
aid, a gentle mentor, to help you formulate and work out
a personal plan to manage your value system. Your success or failure in using that plan to your advantage is your
responsibility; it is yours and yours alone.

Every effort has been made to make this book as complete and accurate as possible. However, there may be mistakes both typographical and in content. Therefore, this
text should be used only as a general guide and not as the
ultimate source of information on the topics contained in
the book.

The purpose of this book is to inform, educate, and
entertain. The author and Copper Cove Publishing shall
have neither liability nor responsibility to any person
or entity with respect to any loss or damage caused, or
alleged to be caused, directly or indirectly by the information contained in this book.

If you do not want to be bound by the previous information, do not purchase, read, or use this book in any way.

Foreword

There's all these books aimed at women, shaming them into thinking they need to read them, how to be the perfect woman for your man, how to attract and keep a man, etc., but you never see men bending over backwards to better themselves and their behavior towards us! Finally my uncle Dennis has written a book to set in the basic values every man should hold to be a better friend, better lover, loving father and just a better stand out citizen.

Women have been fighting to be seen as equals for centuries and it's about time men stepped up to the mark as women have definitely taken over in the 'almost perfect' sector: So guys shape up and find your manners and your morals!

I find a lot in today's society and especially on social networks such as Instagram and Twitter that the young boys of today seem to have not been taught how to respect women, and have no idea how to communicate with them, I don't think all the derogative music out there today helps matters and we have odd role models for them to look up to, who in themselves have no respect or morals towards women. So sometimes it feels like us feminists are banging our heads against a very hard brick wall.

We need to take it back to days of real respect shown by real gentlemen. Reading this book can be a first step in the direction of living a life driven by values, exemplified by manners, and moderated by morals.

Amy Christophers
Falmouth, Cornwall
CEO of EDS Sports
London, England
www.amychristophers.co.uk

Prologue

One day, not so long ago, I posted the following on Facebook: "You have all likely heard of the cliché; 'Out of sight, out of mind.' The rest of the storyline is 'out of mind, out of heart; out of heart, out of life,' quote me if you please." My friend Mike pointed out that I forgot to post the circular ending "out of heart, . . . out of life, out of sight." So the whole line goes "Out of sight, out of mind; out of mind, out of heart; out of heart, out of life; out of life, out of sight." And so it goes with a man's internal value system. If a person never hears of or sees an admirable value in the context of how to live his life, it will not likely enter his mind at crucial points when he interacts with other people. If a value isn't present and near the top of a person's mind, it can't find its way to their heart. Values not present in someone's heart (soul, or his essence of being), won't be demonstrated in their thinking or be demonstrated in their life by way of the daily actions taken or not taken. The end result is a man blind to his lack of values, which are necessary for his own well-being, cheating him of having self-esteem, a sense of self-worth, and the ability to peacefully coexist with everyone else in our civil society. Compare the conscious mind to a computer's processor and emotional memories stored in memory as a person's "heart," as one of the databases that can be referenced before a decision is made or an action is taken. Internalizing a system of values provides that ever-necessary point of reference in the database of someone's mind for every decision every person must make throughout life.

This text presents **twenty-one essential values** that adult men, young adolescent men, and boys can benefit from. If they hold these values within their minds and vet their personal behaviors using these fundamental standards, they can make all human interactions ones with positive and helpful outcomes. These twenty-one values can also be used as guideposts to parents and foster parents for bringing up children "in the way they should go." Although the text's gender trend is aimed at men, in the spirit of equality and equal worth, women and girls benefit from knowing these values, internalizing them, and also by associating admirable values with the type of men they would want in their lives. Wise women can capture these values in their own lives, as well. These values are not necessarily masculine or feminine; they are human. Far too many people—particularly men in our world today as demonstrated in the daily news media—seem to lack moral fiber, personal integrity, and good moral character. However you choose to portray it, far too many men in positions of influence lack having stellar ethical behavior. The world news is rife with stories brought to us because of men who hold no values or attach their actions to "false empty values," which are detrimental to self or harmful to others. From those living in the lowest places in our cities' ghettos to those occupying the highest points in marble-floor office buildings, these values can provide that reference and link of regulation to improve all human interactions.

This book's list is not intended to be exhaustive or the only list of important values for humans of all walks of life to hold. It is, however, a list of essential values necessary for *peaceful and prosperous* interactions within our modern society. Achieving manhood and womanhood requires much more than good looks or genetics, hormone levels, strength, or time. If nothing else, let this text start the public conversation of what a value-filled demonstration of life should look like in our modern age. How should young men aspire to behave? We hold up on public pedestals so many celebrities who are the worst examples of manhood. Sports figures who cheat by using performance-enhancing drugs, beat their wives, and abuse their children; politicians who get caught in a sting for taking bribes; business leaders and boards of directors who cheat stockholders and abuse customers and the environment, as well as take unfair advantage of employees. The bad examples are nearly everywhere. Clergy who abuse children and the weak, and school teachers who abuse students are all constantly replaying in the news as examples—week-after-week and generation after generation of poor public and private behavior. The very fact that bullying and antisocial behavior exists in schools and colleges points to a wretched lack of appropriate values on the part of far too many of our young people. Every day on the news someone who is renowned is behaving badly. Are we to use them as our role models? And who decides, simply because of their celebrity status, that they should be role models for our children and grandchildren? I think not. It's time to reset the bar as to what good and acceptable public behavior is for all men and women, and to stop rewarding bad behavior with notoriety, and even worse, any form of praise, no matter how well they sing, act, play games, or are politic. If it were possible, we should halt rewarding those who behave poorly with our purchases and praise. Even more disdain belongs to advertising executives who push the faces of notoriously bad examples of behavior into our television screens. Accountability on a public scale means not buying, not condoning, and never overlooking gross public behavior, whether it's a notable young woman shoplifting or a young singer drag-racing while intoxicated on our public streets. Bad public behavior that can harm others physically is bad public behavior. Rewarding and aggrandizing those who display such behavior in any way to our younger, more influenceable citizens is ludicrous. Accountability for our value-challenged politicians means no more votes or a recall and, certainly, no more campaign contributions when their rascal qualities brought about by a lack of values become public. Sadly, the fifth estate isn't without those who display belligerent behavior. Poor casting and show-premise choices are made by networks and cable channels where the show's only intent is incitation of those viewers who often seem incapable of original thought and having opinions of their own. The off switch or remote control to change the channel are your only recourse for such antisocial shows. Or, simply boycott the products offered in the ads.

I also want to be clear to the reader. This author doesn't claim to possess all the values presented here to the point of being a perfect person. Perfection isn't possible. We often earn our values through the mistakes we've made when values weren't on the top of our minds. I do want to be clear, though, I do now claim these values as my personal benchmark for my own public and private behavior. I, too, am a work in progress with much room for improvement. Striving for perfect adherence to a system of internalized value isn't only possible, it's mandatory for those determined to do and be better. After reading the values presented here, my hope is that more men, women, boys, and girls will do the same. That is to work on adopting a core value system benefiting self, family, neighborhoods, state, nation, and the entire world society as a whole. This would mean adopting these values (or at least some of them) as a personal benchmark for your own public and private behaviors.

My hope is that parents will use this book in their homes as a values conversation-starter with children of an age of reason. If you don't have this conversation with your children, they will get values anyway, just not from you. And many values learned outside the home will certainly be antisocial in nature.

We have nothing to lose and real tangible benefits to gain if people with positive values, regardless of their station in life, are held in esteem for their value systems, and not only for their fortunes or achievements on any given day. It's time that, we as a society, reexamine the question: **"What measures make a person great: what collective set of values will define personal morality and individual responsibility in our society and world for the rest of this century?"**

In some ways, our language is limited, even with the terms "men" and "women" being interpreted to mean many different things to the speaker or writer, while other ideas are perceived within the hearer or reader. We use words to transfer ideas and, in defining values of real people in the words presented in this text, many associated ideas move and are included, right along with the definitions to aid our understanding. These ideas, if internalized by an individual, govern behaviors as a group of important values with no particular hierarchy, or with one value being more important than another. Stated more simply, no single value should have the power of cancelling another. Just like the ribs and stretchers on an umbrella, each value is of equivalent importance.

So many other written sources—magazines, shows, news, books—all have pontificated on the subject of manhood or womanhood from the concept of a person possessing physical strength, prowess, power, wealth, achievement, and fame that I felt compelled to write this book by looking at values at a more fundamental level. I can admire that we may begin to call a boy a man when he turns 18 or 21, or when he joins the military, goes off to college, or gets his first paying job. I can cheer when a young rodeo rider clocks in his eight seconds on a Brahma bull. What any of us can't know with any certainty is if this new man behave and act in ways that deserve our admiration in his daily activities. This text was written to help improve the odds that the accumulations of acts, behaviors, reactions, and deeds of more people over their lifetimes will deserve our esteem. More importantly, that, you, the reader of this text, will come to earn and deserve our admiration as a kind and gentle person acting out their life before us in ways that intentionally harm no one. These values can begin to build the framework of a dignified life.

Whose job is it to teach values? It's fair to say that many in the potential instructor pool could play a positive role. This includes home, family, schools, colleges, the military, churches, synagogues, community leaders, the news, and parents, many of whom have failed some people miserably and others to a degree where they're only slightly morally corrupt. Many of these roles and institutions can play a positive part, however regrettably they are, at times, espousing marginal value systems leading to increasing the head count of morally challenged and even belligerent individuals. So we know from sociologists that parents, family, and peers are a big influence on a person's values, followed by schools and religion as a child ages. Nonetheless, it's every person's responsibility as a thinking human being to give anchor and passage to their own moral behavior. And, it's the individual's job to develop and adopt their own internal code of ethics and, just as important, to take full responsibility for acting in accordance with that code of ethics. Stop the blame games today and take charge of your own personal behavior, regardless of your upbringing or being raised by one community or another. If you're in a position to influence others, take the job seriously and provide help to those in your sphere of influence to become value-driven individuals.

The problem faced by society when morally corrupt or ethically challenged people hurt others is this: all too often, there's either no will or no mechanism to take those displaying detrimental behaviors to task. Admittedly, a good number are held accountable for a failing grade in the moral-fiber department. Some get noticed by law enforcement and the courts. About 4.6 percent of the US population is in jail or under the control of a parole officer. Obviously, this segment of the population failed to adopt values that served them well enough to keep out of the reach of the legal system. This lack of good character and an absence of displaying positive value-driven behaviors allowed them to cross some lines drawn by society and get noticed by law enforcement. The problem is, plenty of others behaving poorly aren't being reported or getting caught, or they aren't actually breaking any laws with their antisocial attitudes enough to get noticed by law enforcement. I call this group the "other" 4 percent **(The Other 4 Percent)**. More discussion about this group is at the end of the book. The other 4 percent's antisocial attitudes and behaviors are well known by everyone who comes in contact with them. But nothing ever happens to them, unless one of those legal lines is crossed and they actually get noticed and apprehended by law enforcement.

A third "invisible" group exists, not yet particularly noticeable, is one that nonetheless engages in antisocial and criminal behavior. These are the ones who manage to keep their antisocial actions a total secret. These same people may be known by others in society, but they're kept silent and in fear of retribution if they speak out. Domestic abuse and child abuse fall into this category. (This silent group could well be the six-tenths of 1 percent.) This, in some ways, might be the worst kind of behavior as it's under the radar, only known by a few who choose silence over whistle blowing, confrontation, or passing information on to law enforcement. These unnoted individuals are similar to a cancer, a tumor keeping our society from being all it could be. It draws down the good tissue in ways we can't know until it's too late to address with any satisfying adjudication. Regrettably, the lack of visibility giving rise to generation after generation of people who mistakenly believe it's OK or somehow their right to abuse others.

The military is the only entity I know of that can hold its officers to a high standard where anything deemed by the command as poor behavior can have consequences, although it isn't always exercised enough or with consistency across the ranks or all branches of service. Article 133 of the US Uniform Code of Military Justice allows "Conduct unbecoming an officer and gentleman" to be punished by a court martial. Those actions leading to courts martial would include: a failure to exhibit good taste, propriety, or etiquette; indecency; law-breaking; unfair dealings; injustice; or cruelty. Perhaps business and other institutions should copy this page from the military's playbook and hold their operatives accountable to a solid value system inside and outside of the boardroom.

Lessons from history tell about the fate of ill-behaved men since history was first recorded. Heraclitus (540–480 BC) is credited with many translations of his writings that can be summarized by saying that a person becomes the result of the principled choices he makes. A man lacking moral principles is no gentleman, in fact, is not a man at all, in the context of this book.

No one would doubt today from watching the TV news that we have lost at least a few of the details in our collective responsibility of raising our boys in a way that makes them real men. Watch the news on any given night and you can see the results of boys and men being brought up without the very necessary values of being good, kind, and decent men, worthy of respect from other men, women, and children. Excuses for not endowing children with a value system that benefits the child and society as a whole are no longer valid, if those excuses ever were valid. Our society is hurting when bullying is commonplace. Our systems are broken when women can't serve in uniform without being damaged by their male comrades instead of our enemies. Our college campuses aren't a completely safe place for young women to live and study. Young women are sometimes even preyed on by their professors. Our institutions are shown to be lacking of real men when theft, mismanagement, embezzlement, and corruption are rampant, if not commonplace in business and government. An even graver problem is when institutions attempt to sweep crimes in their spaces under the rug and hide behind legal speeches. Our market squares are filled with filthy language and swearing because boys and men can't even take responsibility for moderating their speech in public places, let alone in private environments. Just watch any episode of some of the reality shows on cable or satellite TV, and you'll see men and women with little, if any, beneficial value systems behaving consistently with an absence of appealing moral values. It's a sad commentary on our public and private life when every community of any size needs a battered women's shelter. The examples of men with failed core value systems are found all around us, all too easy to find.

It's way past the time for a change. We can't count on any of our institutions—including schools, colleges, churches, and community clubs—to begin making or demanding these changes and instilling values in our young boys, and young and old men alike. We can't count on the media, be it traditional TV and radio or social media platforms, to begin the dialog. And more than dialog, we need to begin placing worth on men who display values worthy of the mantra of manhood, and denying notoriety or reward of any kind to those who are morally empty and corrupt. I, for one, don't need to see another celebrity in prison-striped or red/orange garb and in custody for, if nothing else, being stupid and immature. We can't count on our politicians or political institutions to call for a return to value-driven behaviors when some of the most egregious behaviors are given life by politicians and in the hallowed halls of our states' senates and houses of representatives. Parents across all economic groups are failing to instill in young boys and men just what it means to be a real man, someone worthy of respect and admiration. *It's time for society to place a worth, not on how strong a man is, but how strongly he is rooted in endearing and socially beneficial values.* If a young man is over the age of reason, he can begin to fix this within himself. He can examine his thinking and past behaviors. He can change the antisocial and antihumanitarian behaviors, as well as those behaviors that are mirrored back in any way to cause damage to self. A reader of this text in a position of being part of the community that brings up a child or children empower yourself into the conversation to make a difference. There is no need to tolerate valueless behaviors, when it is wrong say it's wrong. When you have the opportunity to mentor a young man carefully examine what it is that you are teaching him.

We take our children to sporting events as fans or have them participate where they learn there are winners and losers, as if, somehow, this is all that matters and it applies to all undertakings in life. That winning—regardless—matters the most, is a shallow lesson. Carrying and acting out of gentle characteristics of real manhood doesn't make a man weak or a loser. On the contrary, when you threaten a man's right to hold these values and act out these values, you may suffer justifiable wrath. Even the rules of warfare contain values embodied in the Geneva Convention about the treatment of fellow humans even when they're an enemy. For signature nations, the treaties require maintaining a value system that doesn't abandon the personal dignity of enemy combatants and nonhostiles on the battlefield. Yet, we tolerate behaviors that would be in violation of these treaties by men and boys in our streets. Humiliating and degrading treatment of others is outlawed even in war. In no way should it be permitted in any part of our public life, even in the competitive sports arena. Real men with values controlling their behavior never participate in humiliating and degrading treatment of others, regardless of the team they're on.

*Let's then take a moment to define a **real man** for the purposes of this text. A real man is a male human marked* *with qualities valued by society that are exemplified by his being able to live in peace, one with another. A real man internalizes and displays in his life qualities considered characteristic of manhood, such as what it takes to be a gentile master of his mental powers. A real man conducts himself with moral judgment and controls his behaviors and actions in ways that do no harm to others, either physical harm or mental anguish.* A male person who has lost his senses or acts without good judgment, gives in to immoral, unjust, and illegal behaviors that harm others or himself isn't defined as a real man. We say such a person isn't even his own man. He is behaving less-than human, and he is criticized as behaving and acting more like an animal. Genesis, in the story of creation verses, is presented first in the collective books we call *The Bible* and *The Bible* is a book that contains the information God wanted us to know about Himself. Adam and Eve collectively give in to the desires and instructions of the foe of God and partake of something forbidden. In religion, this is taught as original sin, and the defining message from these ancient verses is that we humans are all capable of doing evil. Every man of sound mind is also capable of and responsible for choosing to do good over evil. Our entire legal system is based on this concept. Men don't normally act contrary to their internal value system. Therefore, it's critical that children, boys, and young men be taught values that can benefit them throughout their lives and that will, in turn, also benefit our human society worldwide. In this book, the text covers and discusses values or characteristics carried by what the text defines as real men.

At the end of a man's life, the question is how will that life be summarized by the people who knew him? If you had a say in the matter, how do you want to be remembered? When my eldest brother Edward passed away, one of his friends summarized Ed's life to me at his funeral by saying "He didn't have much (possessions or wealth), but he had what matters." His friend meant that Ed had what it took to give of himself to others. Anytime someone needed help and Ed knew about it, he was there to be helpful. As a master electrician in business for himself, he would drive 50-plus miles, do complicated electrical repairs for hours for retired people on small fixed incomes, and, at the end of the day, simply charge them for the gas it took to get there and back. Ed did this hundreds of, if not countless, times throughout his life. Ed knew that an outright gift often left the person with less self-esteem, but a $5 charge left them with their problem solved and their dignity intact.

My older brother Paul tells a similar values-held story about our father who passed away shorty after I turned two years old. Paul said he was about eleven or twelve years old and my dad Leslie was teaching him to drive the Ford Model A truck, so he could help out more on the farm. During his first time steering a U-turn in the cows' pasture, Paul—being totally new at the wheel—hit one of the new cedar fence posts. Paul pulled many other posts that were connected to the barbed wire to the ground before he could stop the car. Many fathers might have yelled at their son, but not our dad.

Dad simply looked over at Paul and said, "We are lucky today."

Paul asked, "What do you mean lucky? I just knocked over new fence posts and seriously bent the car's fender!"

Dad replied, "We are lucky. The shovel is in the back of the car, and it will only take us a few minutes to fix this fence and get back to your driving lessons."

Dad bent out the fender, they repaired the fence posts together, and the driving lessons continued, as did the lifelong example of displaying excellent behavior at what could have been a very stressful and angry moment. This moment shaped Paul's own behavior for life.

As a man, young man, or boy in this world, you either set the example for others or will be a bad example for others. There is no neutral position. At times, even silence is often taking a side for good or evil. When you think about it, choosing to display good behavior is really no harder than choosing between white bread and wheat bread. We make these kinds of choices every day. Once a person knows what the behavior bar demands from a real man, and once he has had time to internalize values that give way to behaviors based on closely held values, which are exemplary of manhood, he is much more easily able to choose to act accordingly.

Parents bringing up sons in today's world without a value system that will make endearing men of them is very much tantamount to child abuse. And, yes, you have failed as a parent if your son or sons don't have positive core values that can guide them throughout their lives. If, as a reader, you are already an adult who had the misfortune of growing up in a household where positive values weren't taught or exemplified for you to emulate, then now is the time to learn, internalize, and practice using positive values to govern what is left of the rest of your life. Start right now. Once values are internalized, it's hard to act contrary to them. Doing so causes stress, as well it should. As a parent reading this, you have little time from your child's birth until the first day of preschool to instill values they will take to school and, ultimately, into the world. For, surely, if you don't teach values by the time you send them out, they will come home from school with some values you and our greater society of civilized people wouldn't want them to have and internalize.

The very first rule of using values to govern your life is to first engage your brain. Turn on your thought process and rid yourself of what the common cliché calls knee-jerk reactions. Reactionary thoughts formed in your brain move into your conscious at a speed of about one-half of a millisecond. That second thought (having the better idea) takes the same length of time, but you must first pause long enough to let it materialize. Once your core values are internalized, the correct response to a situation or opportunity can become the first and the right response.

How do you measure up as a good and real man in this twenty-first century? What do your close family, extended family, neighbors, and coworkers think of you? What are your true unfiltered statuses in the groups and associations you belong to? Perhaps, more importantly, what do you think of yourself? If you were given a psychology test measuring your internal values that graded you on likely behaviors considered legal, moral, and just in our society, how would you fair?

If you are a parent or guardian reading this book, please realize that you are bringing up a future member of the club of men. You have a responsibility to the boy and society to instill values that will benefit society as a whole and the lad as an individual as he grows into manhood.

All women, parents or not, share some responsibly for condoning or not condoning anti-social behaviors in men. Looking the other way at behaviors you would portray as character flaws only brings regret. This is particularly true if you subscribe to the philosophy that it takes a community to raise a child. Pushing a child to be tough, mean-spirited, and a bully, because you fear he'll be pushed around by others if you don't, is also a form of child abuse. No matter how tough your kid is, someone tougher will find him anyway. Just look at what happens on the streets of Chicago, when someone isn't tough enough; $50 will buy an equalizer, and that tough kid may need a coffin. It happens about once a day there, as well as in many other cities. Improve your child's chances of survival to adulthood: teach him some values before it's too late.

"When I was a kid, I . . . (whatever)." Have you ever heard someone say that? I have, and I have probably said it myself, too. However, don't lose sight of the fact that you aren't a kid anymore. You may still be somebody's child, but you're now an adult and you should be taking full responsibility for your actions as an adult. Surely, once across the age 18 line, you're fully responsible for your behavior—not your parents' lousy parenting or the bad breaks you had as a kid. It's time to stand up and be counted. And it's time to stop analyzing what kind of parents you may have had or how bad they were at parenting. It's now time to start asking what kind of kid you are or were. For those with living parents, it's time to let them know you now know you weren't a perfectly behaved child and maybe you owe your mom or dad an apology for your own bad behavior. What kind of child are you today? That's the question to ask and answer honestly. On Valentine's Day, it's 85 days until Mother's Day 2015. And it's 42 more days from Mother's Day until Father's Day. That shouldn't matter at all and here's why. For those of us whose parents are no longer within earthly reach, we get it, at least most of us do. Even for us, hindsight has taught that the other 364.25 days each year are the ones that matter the most. There have been many messengers of values over the eons. I am nowhere near the first, beginning with Moses coming down from the mountain with what we now treat mostly as the "Ten Suggestions." It's time to think in terms of hoping—perhaps praying—for a value-driven era. After journeying fourteen years into a new century, maybe it's too late for our families, neighborhoods, nation, and the world. We have collectively tried freedom, drugs, pot, booze, money, religion, and blame (to name a few) so we could step away from the responsibility for our own behaviors. None of those methods truly provides us with the ability to get better with time. Now is the time for honest reflection, forgiveness, and a renewed resolve toward being responsible value-driven adults every day of our lives.

Internal Values
Do Drive Behavior

Many reasons exist that behaviors driven by positive values seem to be missing in our public space, as well as in our public and private conversations, and in media discussions be they broadcast, cable, or print. Poor parenting, popular culture, the media, flash communication on the Internet, and the false promise of humanism have all moved people from around the world away from traditional cultural and religious values. They have moved toward a philosophy that causes people to believe any behavior they can get away with is just fine. Regrettably, all too often, we aggrandize those who are perceived as rebels, lone wolves, or tough guys. Holding positive values and acting within a positive value system solves most problems in human interactions and, ultimately, in society as a whole. However, far too few possess and act out of a set of commendable core values. Visualize, for a moment, families where everybody gets along; neighborhoods are void of vandalism and theft; shopping malls are free of crime; classrooms are free of bullies; open, honest, and fair governments exist at all levels; there are businesses where customers are given fair value in product and service for the price they pay; and employees and managers alike share only in the relative value they actually add to the business. Imagine that a reduction in the number of criminal court cases could start a downward spiral across the country. Picture a world where countries find ways to cooperate to better the lives of their own citizens and the lives of everyone on the planet.

Perhaps, in every way, this vision of a value-driven society is a day dream or a pipe dream never to become a reality. If this is true, then why continue reading? Here's why. Continue reading because of the worth of one. Become that one more person who can be added to the ranks of those living a value-driven existence. Keep reading because you want to mentor someone else to be that one more person. Become that one more person who can be a positive role model in every sphere you enter. Self-esteem is an impossible goal for those who live a life void of positive values. The reality is that actions—good or evil—are mirrored back to a person doing the actions. No one ever really respects a thief, a batterer, an abuser, a hot head, a vandal, a rapist, or any other nefarious villain of any stature. Children, adolescents, and men who act badly toward others can't expect to be treated well or be well-thought of by others. Become the person others can respect because you are a person driven and supervised by your own internal core value system.

In the next twenty-one segments of this book, admirable core values are defined in an appropriate way to allow them to model and govern behaviors during your interactions with others. It is said that new behavioral habits take twenty-one days to internalize. Read these sections and honesty evaluate if you hold the value discussed in that section. In the event that you come up lacking a value you consider worth owning, work on it for twenty-one days. Read that section the first thing in the morning. Find ways to act out that value in your relationships and daily interactions. Tape a label with that value written on it to your coffee cup or soft drink, so with every sip, you're reminded of that value many times a day for those twenty-one days. Write a paragraph or two or three on ways that you can modify your behavior and reactions with that new value when confronted with circumstances that would have caused you to act differently in the past. By "act differently," I mean failing to engage in true problem-solving behavior. Substituting one problem for another also isn't considered problem-solving behavior. Ask family members or peers to remind you daily about the value you're trying to capture into your core value system. Try one of these techniques or others of your liking to help you focus your conscious and sub-conscious mind on, including this new value in your decision-making process. Find and use a technique that works for you. Internalizing twenty-one values taking twenty-one days each will take four-hundred and forty-one days, almost a year and three months of effort . . . less time if you already own some of these values in your core value system.

When mentoring others, such as a child or stepchild, nephew or neighbor, or mentee, read the section in the book to them and find ways to discuss it every day for twenty-one days. Use what-if questions, examples, or stories from your own experience to help younger people understand and internalize the value into their decision-making development.

True problem-solving behavior only occurs when positive value-driven choices rule over our every behavior and help determine every goal we try to achieve.

Truth

What is truth? *Truth conforms to reality. True defines as what is real, not false. Truth is bilateral, necessary in both directions in human interactions.*

No one likes being lied to; lies cause damage to the teller and the receiver. The liar compromises his integrity and the hearer is devalued. Truth isn't always pretty or kind. At times, telling or receiving the truth is a painful, but necessary, step in human relationships.

Being truthful begins with knowing who you are and accepting who you are. Puffery and pride in oneself is the basis of all deceit. Begin holding the trait of honesty by being truthful with yourself about all aspects of your own character. Consider what values you think you hold and demonstrate in your dealings with others and our environment. If you don't like who you are, change who you are . . . change what you don't like. Don't deceive yourself and others to appear in public or private as a character you aren't.

A real man is truthful in his relationships with all others. Appreciate the full value of truth.

Be truthful in your business dealings and at work, regardless of the culture you're in. Good bosses can accept the untarnished truth and good subordinates respect a leader who is truthful with them.

Moses brought this value down from the mountain and codified it for all time. No one today can claim originality on this important value, but we can all own it and make it a part of our mantra for living an honest life.

Lies are told in so many ways in our politically correct society today, it's often hard to cipher out the truth. Wrong word choices, spin, and commentary that avoids the core issue all contribute to sidestepping the truth. Keeping silent with the purpose of allowing others to make invalid assumptions—and acting on those false assumptions when you know they aren't true—is also being deceitful.

You must be truthful in your witness to others. Don't repeat things unless you know they are true. So many hoaxes and some downright lies are passed around today on the Internet, as well as through various social media. Passing on information from others about others is called gossip. The operative element about gossip is that the information may or may not be true. Truthful people never act on hearsay (gossip as it would be called in a courtroom) and they don't repeat such information to others.

It's important to be truthful to yourself about your own feelings. Above all else, a man is truthful, first with himself, and then others.

Silence is a preferred action if you're tempted to tell lies or misrepresent facts in any circumstance. Only one moral justification exists for a lie: if it will save a life or prevent physical harm to another person.

Often people will say "I'll try" when they really mean "no." Don't concern yourself about others' feelings. No means no. Be honest. In the long run, this is a better policy. Using the word "try" in your answer to a question is a euphemism for "I don't think you can handle my saying 'no.'" That is more offensive to the hearer than tactfully speaking the truth and saying no, when you have no real intention of trying.

When you receive information from others on a matter of importance always, always delay acting on it until you can check out the information for yourself. In government and business circles this is called *vetting,* checking out data for its truthfulness.

All other values are impossible to fully internalize and exemplify in your life without honesty.

Maxim #1: Always speak truthfully.

Learning

What is learning? *Learning is acquiring knowledge, experience, and skill. It is much more than schooling or taking courses, although that is often the best shortcut to new knowledge. Learning involves reading, practicing, and testing information. It is reflection on experiences, as well. Learning also involves taking lessons from your own mistakes and the mistakes of others.*

A man values learning and, rather than trying to get by with simply applying what he knows to his work product, he also endeavors to learn from each new event or experience. He attempts to gain insight though critical evaluation. He adds to his own wisdom by comparison to other experiences in life and learns from others' mistakes. You don't have enough time to make every possible mistake on your own. A man believes that life-long learning is an important factor in the quality of his own life. By learning, I don't mean watching what passes for news on the Fox TV channel and being told what you should think by people who probably aren't any smarter than you. Read books, look up words in the dictionary, check encyclopedias for information on topics that interest you.

On the topics that interest you most, read and study all you can about them—read everything available. This is, indeed, how experts on a subject are created. Students who complete twelve grades of high school are in class about 180 days a year. They sit in classrooms somewhere near six-and-a half hours each day, for a total of less than the equivalent of only 1,755 equivalent eight-hour work days, less than five equivalent work years. Yet, with this small amount of time in class, we consider the high school graduate ready for higher learning. It isn't enough education for the vast majority of people to be prepared to excel in anything. Most apprenticeships require four years at 2,080 hours per year, for a total of 8,320 hours where you are focused entirely on learning a trade or skill. After high school, after college, even after achieving a PhD, you aren't fully prepared for all of the challenges you will face in life or a career. You must dedicate an amount of time every day to learning new things. Strengthen your brain by using it and by becoming better prepared for excellence in your job, profession, or vocation. No matter what your station in life, you can learn things that will make you better at all you do, whatever that may be. As a parent, educate yourself on parenting. Don't just think you can figure out how to be the best possible parent for each of your children. Use education to become the one who excels in your chosen work field. Use financial education sources for meeting the economic challenges you might face. Study human behaviors to learn how to interact better with others. Become a critical thinker using your education to find patterns and similarities, to compare and contrast information from one topic to another, and to find new applications for the patterns you recognize.

Set new learning goals for yourself every seven years. Write down those goals in ways that make them easy to relate to. For example, it wouldn't be unreasonable for a seven-year-old to set a goal of graduating from high school by age 14. Nor would it be unreasonable for a high school graduate to set a goal of having a PhD in seven years or less. Education goals don't have to be that lofty, but you must have them in writing and act on achieving them every day in some way.

Staying ignorant to new knowledge is such a life-limiting comportment; it nearly equals the total waste of a life. Your brain can be at rest, it can be sleeping, lost in daydreams, but limiting the information it has to work with is a life-limiting mistake made by far too many people. You hear excuses, such as "I was bored," "I never liked school," and so on. The point is you aren't in school that much time. You need to take on the responsibility to find and learn the information that can make your life better. Become capable of making the lives of the ones you love better through increased learning. Only you can decide what information that needs to be, so get busy and explore topics that interest you most.

How much time is enough to excel? Students in elementary, middle, high school, and even in college can often excel simply by beating the study time average of their peers. By that, I mean finding out what the average time is that their peers spend on studying each subject, and beating the average time by fifteen to thirty minutes per subject. This involves reading the extra credit information, going over your own work for accuracy, and reading all the extra reference material. Each person's brain can only absorb so much information at a time, so the only variable that can be improved on is dedicating and using more time in learning the subject matter.

Always striving for personal knowledge growth will improve your life in ways that are impossible to predict.

Maxim #2: Open your mind
and seek new knowledge every day.

Leadership

What is leadership? *Leadership is far more than just positional authority. Leadership is the act of causing yourself, one other person, a group, an organization, a company, or a country to accomplish pre-defined positive goals and objectives with measurable and verifiable results.*

You may have heard the old adage to "lead, follow, or get out of the way," which is attributed— rightly or wrongly—to the American patriot Thomas Paine. What I refer to as "owning leadership" as a manly quality involves being the first one to get up and get going on what needs to be done. A leader doesn't need to be told or ordered to do something; neither does he need to delay to follow the lead of others. A leader in any situation is the one who moves him and the group, if there is one, in the direction of getting things done. A leader sees a need for turning productive thoughts and plans into actions and begins taking action to achieve a worthy goal, no matter how large or small it may be.

A leader tells people what he wants from them with no room for misunderstanding. We see failures in leadership every day. All you have to do is watch the news.

As I was finishing this manuscript, the President of the United States was on TV a few times to pontificate about the events in Ferguson, Missouri. He was in a unique position to say what needed to be said as a leader, but he failed to do so. Recently, some military leaders—now retired—admitted to their leadership failures in the recent arduous skirmishes in Iraq, Afghanistan, and in the fights with terrorists all over the globe it seems.

A leader also sets the standard by his own good examples, his own actions, and his commendable performance. A leader internalizes and uses many, if not all, the values in this book for metering his actions and interactions with others in his sphere of influence and in the world.

Leaders make decisions every day to make things better in the world for everyone they come in contact with. Evil people and criminals can be leaders, but for what purpose? As a leader, your responsibility is to build others up, not to tear anything good down or do harm.

Leadership can be learned both through academic study and through thoughtful experiences. Both channels to become a true leader require an equal amount of work.

Lead if you are able. If you aren't able to lead, follow only those you can respect until you're able to take the lead yourself.

Maxim #3. Appreciate good leadership qualities in others and cultivate them in yourself.

Note: The Dennis the Mentor™ series has already published a quick read focused entirely on leadership called Dennis the Mentor ™ *Cover Your Six Leadership.* Available from BarnesandNoble.com, on Amazon as hard copy or Kindle, and in fine book stores everywhere.

Perseverance

What is perseverance? *Perseverance as a value is pushing though the many temptations to quit on the way to a goal. It is steadfastly sticking to achieving goals, regardless of the difficulties or delays faced along the way.*

Along with not-starting-at-all, quitting-too-soon is a common problem. This results in mediocre success or not achieving any positive performance record at all. Pulling away from a goal before you've had the chance to find personal growth from the experiences of trying hard results in little, if any, reward.

An hour. What's in an hour? Let's do the math. If you live to be 100 years old, which most of us won't, we would have from birth to death (365.25 days times 100 yielding 36,525 days). Multiply by twenty-four hours in each day, which gives us only 876,600 hours in a lifetime. Dying at age 65 leaves a person with only 569,790 hours of available time. Time, that next hour, is given to nearly all of us in the same measure. Unless you're one of the 6,500 people on the planet who perish every hour, you're given the next hour in equal measure to everyone else on the planet. But, much like the crusader's warning, we must choose wisely as to what is done with that hour. We can use those hours or waste them. Real men choose to use them, and they use them for good, legal, and moral purposes. Persevering toward your goals is partly about not wasting that time you're given every day.

A real man maintains an attitude of perseverance toward achieving reasonable goals based in moral standards and positive values. A man turns away from valuable challenges only when success has proven impossible. Giving up, quitting too soon, or not starting at all are synonymous with the personal tragedy of unnecessary failure.

Perseverance must manifest itself in at least four areas of your life. First, some things are hard to do in the physical arena. You must exercise muscles or they will diminish over time. Second, the brain is no different. Some logical connections are hard to make or learn without effort. Mental acuity comes from working through mental challenges until understanding is found. Third, humans have a need for perseverance in spiritual matters as well; believing in something is more than a one-time effort. And, fourth, the same is true in emotional matters. Some attention to emotional wellness of self and the others you love and care about requires daily actions. You need to constantly seek improvement in those relationships.

Worthwhile tasks and goals are worthy of your persistent efforts.

Maxim #4. Stick with your goals
or you will be stuck by your failures.

Diligence

What is diligence? *Diligence is treating every task you undertake with a steady effort and careful attention to every detail to be thorough and accurate, and to follow the task through to completion.*

You could argue that everything in life is not worthy of grade *A* work. Some things are good enough for only a *C* earning effort and some tasks merit only a checkmark as done. Nothing could be further from the truth. Leave mediocrity to others and always give every job or task you sign up for the effort and attention it deserves. Sure enough, doing your best work often takes more time. Paying attention to quality takes more time and effort. Being complete and thorough always takes more time. Taking enough time up-front often prevents wasting time by having to go back and correct mistakes, or dealing with the sometimes severe consequences of errors or omissions. Being diligent in all your endeavors eliminates the need to defend your effort or making excuses for failures and blunders later on.

Strive to always be the person who can be counted on for getting the details right.

Maxim #5: Never give any half-efforts:
thoroughly complete every undertaking.

Faith

What is faith? *Faith is an unquestioning confidence that a creator God exists. It is trusting that your life has an import-ant purpose or role in a divine plan to make your life and the lives of others meaningful.*

There is a God, who is the creator of all things, whether you want to believe it. Spending any of your life's energy arguing the existence of God, denying the existence of God, or trying to prove or disprove the existence of God is a com-plete waste of time and energy. We are, simply put, human. We don't know everything or understand everything about the planet we live on, let alone the vast universe our planet occupies. Not to have faith or a belief in a power outside of himself places a man in the position of being godlike unto himself. Nothing good can come from a person carrying and believing in the mistaken idea that no reckoning or accounting exists for his behavior in this life or the next.

Even if you think a creator God is a total myth, then deluding yourself into believing there is one—even if this thought or idea is beyond your reasoning ability—you'll find that believing a creator God exists can lead you to live a better life. I do not intend to convince you of this or to try to convert you to a particular brand of faith or religion in this text. I am simply presenting to you, regardless of your religious beliefs, affiliations, or lack thereof, that having faith is a valuable feature in man. And men who have faith in God are more prone to display positive social behaviors, to think of the well-being of others, and to act in humility. If you're a person without faith in God, and if you're hung up on logic and reason, here is some indisputable logic for you: you can only find out if you were right or wrong about a creator God, and heaven and hell after your own death, so reporting back to the rest of mankind will be impossible for you.

Those individuals who behave in anti-social ways are often reported to "find religion" after long periods of incarceration in prison. I suppose that long periods of isolation and time to do nothing much more than think might have some bearing on the phenomenon of jail-house conversions.

A real man believes that life should be lived in the presence of God in a manner that reflects a never-ending appreciation for both our earthly blessings and our daily challenges, great and small.

A life lived in a state of disbelief in the divine is a life empty of eternal purpose.

Maxim #6: Have faith (believe) there is a God whose wisdom created each of us, and who possesses power and knowledge beyond human understanding.

Friendship

What is friendship? *Friendship as a value is maintaining the attitude that all others should be treated with kindness. Friendship is always treating those people close to you with trust and respect.*

Real men accept and embrace the idea that the quality of his own life is reflected in the depth and breadth of loving relationships with friends and family. A man works at nourishing and cherishing those relationships with the friends and family he has. He treats the new people he encounters as potential new friends.

The quality of the people you chose as friends will, especially for young people, shape many of your moral values, especially in areas that haven't been taught to youth and adolescents during formative years at home. Peer pressure presents the potential for positive personal growth, as well as an equal potential for learning dangerous behaviors and accepting negative anti-social ideas. Save your friendship for people you can respect and who are respected by others for their sound moral behaviors.

Parents often seek exclusive education for their children in charter schools and the best parochial schools on the premise that the child will get a better education. Along with that education comes a certain amount of peer pressure from the "cool" kids in the group. All too often the cool kids are coddled, overindulged, smug, and entitled, with access to money and drugs. They can be examples of immorality, entitlement, and abusive behavior toward others. Teach children to be discerning when it comes to choosing their friends. If someone is deserving of your friendship, their behaviors should never require you to make up excuses for them.

Choose friends who build up you and others.

Maxim #7: Nourish your friendships every day with kind words and caring actions.

Forgiveness

What is forgiveness? Forgiveness is the act of not punishing or holding anyone who has ever grieved or harmed you in any way in disfavor. Forgiveness is excusing them from any consequences of every transgression against you. Forgiveness is the polar opposite of revenge.

Revenge is not sweet. At best, all revenge does is multiply the number of wronged parties. Being forgiven for your errors and forgiving others is the foundation for peace (peace of mind, peace of spirit, or peace of God) in your own life. Without forgiving those who have wronged you, and without seeking forgiveness from others, that coveted peaceful existence will always evade you. Begin by forgiving yourself for past mistakes. Then, forgive others who wronged you and let them know you have done so. You and others may well be guilty of grievous errors and wrongdoing, each may suffer consequences for mistakes made, but forgiveness removes the condemnation.

Freedom from guilt and punishment is the seed from which grows all future happiness.

Maxim #8: Holding a grudge past sundown
darkens the soul.

Diversity

What is diversity? *Diversity is recognizing that humankind is composed of people from differing social status, genetics, backgrounds, ethnicities, talents, and intelligence, yet still valuing them as having equal worth.*

We aren't all equal, no matter what the measure. Some people run faster, others can do complex math in their head, some are tall, and some are short. I could go on making hundreds of similar comparisons. The adage that "all men are created equal" isn't true in every sense that some people want to apply it. The truth is, we are all different and the refrain should be that "all people are of equal worth and should be treated as equally valued members of the human race." We are all different with differing abilities, talents, strengths, weaknesses, and varying degrees of accomplishments. We are a diverse human race. It may be just a few genes that separate us from all other people and from group-to-group. None are less valuable than the other because of a gene difference that makes one person's hair black and another's blond. None are less valuable than the other because their skin is red or black, and mine is white based on a change in one pair of genes. If the finding from the science of genetics is correct in its basic assumptions that all of us now alive on the planet have descended from a single genetic "Eve," and are descended from very few men making us all distant cousins of sorts at some level.

A real man values diversity in race, nationality, heritage, and thought. A real man believes everyone should be valued for the positive contributions their uniqueness and contributions present to the body of human thought and knowledge, as well as the useful things they can bring to fruition to benefit others. The color of his hair or her skin shouldn't matter. There is no room for hatred of others solely based on their genetically expressed differences from the outward physical expressions and characteristics of a person's genetic makeup. If you must find something to hate, then hate bad behaviors, and then find pity instead for those who relentlessly engage in antisocial behaviors.

Appreciate that a person's differences can potentially contribute to the betterment of society.

Maxim #9: Discriminate only against evil deeds done or illegal behaviors in others.

Modesty

What is modesty? Modesty is being totally disinclined to boast about your accomplishments, importance, wealth, or general worth. Modesty is the act of staying quiet and not drawing attention to yourself through speech, behaviors, or dress.

A man acting modestly seems to run counter to our culture, yet at the same time, no one likes a braggart. Self-confidence—quiet self-confidence—leads to modesty. Characteristics leading to arrogance, self-aggrandizement, and self-importance are all derived from a lack of modesty and, often, reflect underlying feelings of inferiority.

The best example I can give here is what I call some-one prone to "bar talk." Any bar or tavern you enter likely has someone in it who has been everywhere, done every-thing, and will tell you war stories about his heroic time in the military. But, if you could examine his service record, you wouldn't be surprised to find he only served at the Pentagon and never stepped out of the Washington DC beltway while on duty. Then, there are others who fill the bar with too much information about his lifelong con-quests of women, beginning with the prom queen. Don't be surprised to find later that the happenings were only in his dreams. And there are those who have hunted and killed every animal real or mythical, including the unicorn. You get the idea. The problem is the propensity to be jabbering and engaging in bar talk, which can be on any topic. You are just as likely to encounter bar talk at work or anywhere people congregate.

Being modest doesn't mean you can't be an achiever or famous. It simply regulates how you respond to and use that fame or those achievements.

Let others sing your praises from the basis of your solid accomplishments and contributions to the common good.

Maxim #10: Act in endless humility
to achieve distinction.

Sensitivity

What is sensitivity? *Sensitivity is constantly being aware of and understanding the potential fragility of someone else's feelings. Sensitivity is never acting or speaking in ways that can diminish the feelings or self-worth of another individual or group.*

You can go through this life impervious to the plight and needs or feelings of others. Seeing others in need, fear, helplessness, homelessness, or in need of comfort doesn't really hurt you. Being a real man requires that you become aware of the emotions and feelings of others, and, at the very least, don't take actions to make life worse for someone in plight or need.

Any point where you raise your voice in a conversation you have lost your claim to sensitivity. Avoid using insults in jest or in a somber way. Permanent damage to others can be done with words alone.

Being sensitive translates to never doing harm to others, either physically or emotionally, who are innocent.

Maxim #11: Always display kindness when you show disagreement with another person.

Creativity

What is creativity? *Creativity is the ability to make new things, products, or concepts from new and original ideas.*

A real man believes that creativity, not competition, is the substance or essence from which problems are solved and abundance is found. A man endeavors to encourage the expression of creativity in himself and in others. Competition by design creates winners and losers, leading to fewer choices for all of us. It is a situation where every player in the game is a little worse off, leading to a downward spiral for everyone involved.

The shows *Shark Tank* and *Dragon's Den* are prime examples of how creativity can lead to the creation of wealth. In my observations from viewing the show the sharks tend to avoid investments in highly competitive products and businesses.

Even in social settings, creativity is better. Could anyone stand to read a Facebook posting longer than a paragraph or two? I wonder how literary this international venting venue can be. I tire of the reposting and rehashing of thought, correctly or incorrectly, attributed to the famous. Personally, I savor the originality, insight, and humor provided by those less known, but more connected to life as it really is (or should be) in this nation, and on this spaceship we share on our journey though the cosmos. It's fantastic that we can sometimes be inside the circle of agreement on a topic. But those individuals who step outside the circle of the known and the comfortable with no ill intent or self-serving motive are the ones who move us in a new direction, to a new product, or to an innovative solution to a problem.

Consider all forms of creative endeavors as necessary to enhance the state of humankind and to advance the march of time toward a more perfect world.

Maxim #12: Work to advance the greater good
through creativity in yourself and others.

Contribution

What is contribution? *Contribution is a selfless gift of time, energy, or talents to benefit the common good or other individuals.*

Real men live to seize opportunities to make a positive and helpful contribution to others and to society as a whole. "How can I be useful in this situation?" is the question they ask themselves. When answered, they act on making the contribution to whatever circle of influence they are in at the time. Examples might be asking a question in a classroom. The simple sharing of an experience can help someone else learn a lesson. Cleaning the dishes off the table, even though you're a guest in the house, is a small example. You don't need to solve the world's problems of our time to have the spirit of contribution within. A real man recognizes that God, the natural world, and the whole of society and all mankind worldwide are due his loving gifts out of pure gratitude for his own space and place in this time. These gifts are given as a portion of his time, talent, and treasure for the benefit of others.

Contributing to the well-being of others, even in the smallest way, is the most personally empowering action you can undertake.

Maxim #13: Build up others and yourself by living a life ruled by a generosity of spirit.

Collaboration

What is collaboration? Collaboration is the willingness to work productively and creatively with one or more people to attain the highest quality results.

Let's face facts here, collaboration can be positive or negative. Criminal gangs collaborate, as do traitors and other evil doers of all kinds. So, the value is in the type of collaboration and its intended results, not in the mere fact that a man is willing to collaborate with others. The other negative is that collaboration—expressed in committees, teamwork, and social groups—can often lead to the groups' endorsement of an outcome that is the lowest common denominator, which is the least useful or easiest to achieve outcome. The value we're talking about here is more the willingness to collaborate for the common good and for the best possible outcomes.

A real man is willing to accept the idea that good ideas aren't exclusive to self. He is open to the ideas and suggestions of others and he places worth on the contribution of others. He also values their willingness to collaborate, so together, positive outcomes can result from the group efforts. A real man attempts to add value, when and wherever possible, to the efforts of others in his sphere of influence. It boils down to a real man's behavior in a group, nearly any group. Men absorbed with the value of collaboration know they aren't always right or that they have the best or only answer to a problem. If something is expressed that doesn't make sense, they realize it might be a communication issue—not that the person speaking is crazy or less intelligent, or that their ideas are less valuable. Taking the time to hear what others are saying and fully understanding their point-of-view is essential to collaboration. To exercise this value, the necessary valve turns off the propensity to formulate your next statement and, instead, to listen to and understand the other person's statements. A real man has the willingness to ask gentle questions for more clarification, rather than challenging the person who is sharing ideas.

Creative cooperation can bring about excellent solutions to problems, construct a flawless product, or lead to the best possible outcome of an activity.

Maxim #14: Strive to work well with others
and you will realize unexpected rewards.

Encouragement

What is encouragement? Encouragement is the act of cheering for others to meet their goals or overcome challenges. Encouragement is about inspiring self-assurance and courage in others, as well as in your own undertakings.

A real man first values giving encouragement to others, and he appreciates encouragement from others. A real man encourages others toward their legal, moral, and just goals, and he compliments others at every opportunity for their best work efforts. He is thankful to others for the encouragement received from others for his efforts toward achieving personal goals.

It amuses me that we have praise for critics, yet cheer leaders often go unrewarded. At some level, we all need encouragement. Some people are strong enough to find an overwhelming reason from within to press on with a major undertaking or endeavor, yet others need constant encouragement for the smallest efforts. Everyone can appreciate and benefit from a kind, encouraging word. Even a simple-"thank you" for the work you do can make a difference for someone working toward a goal.

Words of encouragement are similar to sharp chisels that have the power to shape lives and futures.

Maxim #15: Never criticize the noble efforts of others.

Gratitude

What is gratitude? Gratitude is a state of mind where you are full of thankfulness and appreciation for your time and place on this Earth. You are grateful for the abilities that enable you to make a positive contribution to family, friends, and community, as well as to all of humanity.

You often meet people who are never happy. We say their glass is only half-full. These folks are half-empty. They are neither satisfied nor pleased that they're alive at a wonderful point in human history. Being alive and relatively well physically and health wise should, by itself, be cause for some celebration. A life lived in a state of gratitude is a fuller life.

No matter what your station in life, regardless of your net worth, no matter what your health, you are currently enjoying the gift of life. A real man is forever and always thankful to the Creator for the abundance in the universe. A real man is thankful for every conscious moment and the creativity found in himself and others. He is thankful for the potential in himself and each of us to find inner peace. He responds to that peace by being kind and respectful to all people and the planet we live on. Gratitude means being thankful for every element of your life. The resources you have, the people who consider you a friend, your family, and even the financial, physical, mental, and emotional challenges you face. All these and more are cause for having the value of gratitude. Each challenge shapes you and provides you with an opportunity to grow and learn, and helps you become a positive example for others.

A life lived without gratitude builds a sour soul.

Maxim #16: Appreciate everything that just being alive brings your way.

Respect

What is respect? Respect is the act of valuing other people as having worth equal to or exceeding your own. Self-respect is a regard for your own value to self and society.

A real man respects his mother, father, his elders in general, women, children, self, and the laws of his state and nation. A child should be safe to aspire to develop. I saw a father at a big box store (no one likes them, but everyone seems to shop there anyway) verbally abuse his ten-year-old son. The child was clowning around and had locked his dad out of the van in the parking lot on a cold morning. After this happened, I thought that after the outburst, it was too bad the kid couldn't lock his father out of his life. Children aren't any different than any other human. Sometimes, you have to earn a child's respect, too.

Not every person who deserves a man's respect is going to earn it. They are due it anyway. Real men grant a degree of respect to those in positions of authority, which they deserve for the role they play in leading. A real man also grants that same degree of respect to all people and to our environment.

Respect as a core value must extend to include respect for the rule of law and for the rules of the road. This also extends to respect for those in authority, including the politicians of the other political party that you didn't vote for.

Showing respect for self is expressed in your manner of living where you avoid overeating, excessive consumption of alcohol, and the abuse of prescription and street drugs.

It's a sad day when fans wave at and support a celebrity when they get out of jail after a DUI, which many people would rephrase to "attempted or potential" vehicular homicide.

Just recently, I saw a news clip about a New York congressman who demanded "respect" from a reporter, yet after the interview, he threatened to "break him in half." Mr. Congressman (and, you, the reader) respect flows in both directions. If you aren't willing to give it, don't expect to get it from others. The lack of civility in our nation and world is a tragedy brought on by men and more than a few women who lack the moral value of respect for all others. Regrettably for our nation, many of those lacking civility and an admirable internal value system have been elected to positions of power and influence.

Many civil problems and protests have risen simply from a lack of respect in men—a lack of simple human decency toward one another. A lack of respect for the law, law and order in general, and a lack of respect for the community and the people who live in it are often the root cause of civil unrest. Such was the unrest in Ferguson, Missouri.

It appeared to me while I was watching the coverage that the US media forgot what "law enforcement" means. Or, did they never know? I wondered. By definition, it can't be a crime for a police officer to enforce the law. Break the law and the law will be enforced. It's that simple. As a mostly law-abiding citizen, I find all the news coverage defending, martyrizing, and glorifying criminal behavior is enough to turn my stomach. No matter what your color or heritage, if you can't get on your knees in a church for a few minutes a week to seek a contrite life, then by all means get on your knees for a few moments when you're confronted by a law officer. Odds are, if you do either, your instant trip to the pearly gates will be delayed by your own actions. That badge the officer is wearing is tied tightly to a thread that weaves itself through to include every level of government, every elected official past and present, and the entire body of law that defines our rights, responsibilities, and freedoms as citizens. By not showing respect to that officer and his badge, you are showing contempt and disdain for your own well-being along with everyone in your community.

Respect and self-respect are two sides of the same coin, never to be squandered or lost.

Maxim #17: Show complete respect in all you do for others, the laws of the land, and the environment.

Responsibility

What is responsibility? *Responsibility is accepting the consequences and rewards of your behavior. Responsibility also presents a duty to always act out of kindness toward others.*

A real man takes full responsibility for his actions—even for his mistakes, better yet, especially for his mistakes—and he blames no other person or divine providence for his own bad behaviors, foul deeds, or failures.

Taking responsibility begins when you can say with sincerity, "I made a mistake, let me do what is possible to fix the problem. I did it. The problems are problems I caused, so let me take the steps to repair the damage." Being responsible means never blaming others for your own mistakes and misfortune.

On the self-reliance side, responsibility means pulling your own weight, caring for yourself and your family, and not being a constant burden to others.

An irresponsible life is void of true rewards.

Maxim #18: Understand that, without exception,
only you deserve credit or blame
for your actions or inactions.

Restraint

What is restraint? *Restraint is consciously controlling and keeping your responses and reactions to physical or verbal actions or threats directed against you under rational control. Restraint is taking the time to estimate the consequences of your reaction to avoid regret from inappropriate knee-jerk behaviors later. Restraint is taking those few seconds to be sure your response is a problem-solving one, which doesn't create new and worse problems for you and those with whom you're interacting.*

The line between hero and coward, and the line between rage and restraint, both are measured in microseconds. Everyone experiences fear, and everyone, at times of great stress, is prone to rage. What makes a real man a hero is not letting the fear overcome thoughtful action. The same is true of restraint. Essentially, restraint is not letting the sensation of rage overcome more a thoughtful action or inaction, or if the circumstances warrant taking no action. Striking out at the innocent with hurtful words, insults, or physical blows is never warranted. This is both bully and cowardly behavior.

As a society, we expect restraint from police and other law enforcement. We have often been disappointed with the consequences of some officers and citizens who failed to show sufficient restraint to fully assess the risk facing them. A parent damaging a child or another family member, who poses no risk to them, is much worse. It's also sad when disagreements at the workplace lead to violence. We call this "thoughtless behavior" when we see or hear of it. So, think of this adage or meme attributed to many, which involves using the soap box, the ballot box, the jury box, and the bullet box to enforce our rights and resolve our differences. When reacting from a position of restraint, first ask, "Can we talk about this?" If the answer is "No," then determine if a vote is in order for the circumstances. If not, ask if a group can be assembled to mitigate the differences? If not, then, and only then, an aggressive reaction might be warranted.

Restraint is the only behavior that can save you from future shame.

Maxim #19: Let some time engage your brain
before you speak or act. Think, assess,
and then act, in that order.

Risk

What is risk? *Risk is the potential that your expended effort and time or financial investment in something won't reward you at all. Or, it might not reward you to the desired degree you expected when you began the investment of energy, time, or money, or perhaps all three.*

Taking reasonable and responsible risks is a natural part of life. Success from risk-taking that goes well leads to our collective progress as humans. A real man knows that personal growth and new knowledge can come from the fruits of his personal failures and mistakes, as much as from his successes. We aren't talking about a lottery-type risk here. We're talking about the willingness to try to achieve, to be the best at something you can be. We're talking about accepting the risk that failure could, and will, occur at times. Every investment might not pay off. Evaluate the risks beforehand and perform your due diligence to understand the dangers, along with the potential rewards.

Letting fear of taking risks or fear of failure rule your decision-making process will certainly limit your ability to achieve and succeed.

Maxim #20: Never let unsubstantiated fears
prevent you from attempting to achieve
your goals and objectives.

Success

What is success? *Success is achieving positive results, goals, and rewarding outcomes from the direct result of your own efforts.*

We are all cast into various roles during our life. A person should value success in all those roles. He must be willing to work and act out the steps for success in each of the roles. Success doesn't only translate to mean being rich or famous, although it can. Success involves being the best father, the best son to a single mother, the best boyfriend, the best husband you can be. It means being the best employee and giving a good day's work for a day's pay. Whatever roles you carry in your life demand that you be successful at them. I'm not talking about perfection here. Some roles and tasks can be successfully accomplished with an item checkbox, what was expected was done as promised. In other cases, success means real hard work, our very best effort to earn an *A* grade from the role recipient. Being content at being a so-so employee or a so-so wife or husband are examples of not being in the role for full success. You should never be content to be the person whose ship of dreams never arrives at the dock because no effort was ever made to send it out to sea.

Even when doing thankless work, a successful person still always does the best job they are capable of doing. Ending the day or shift knowing you have given full value to what you are doing makes a sufficient reward.

Maxim #21: Become notably successful by doing at least one thing well that benefits others.

The Other 4 Percent: Recognizing Men Void of Values

Once, while working in an environment where responsibility, integrity, courage, and dedication were the published values for members of the organization, I quickly learned that some of the group members didn't display those values in their dealings with others. After many bad experiences, I found that about four out of one hundred displayed downright anti-social behaviors in their dealings with others and with those in authority. This set me to wonder and research why this might be. What I found was interesting in itself. In the United States, a little over 4 percent of the population is either in prison, under the control of a parole officer, or awaiting prosecution for a misdemeanor or felony. It quickly occurred to me that another 4 percent ought to be in prison, on parole, or in line for a trial for their anti-social acts and shameful behavior. The people I met whose conduct was the worst made me wonder how they had avoided the reach of the legal system thus far.

Men and women who lack a majority of these values are the ones in our society, and world for that matter, who become a member of what I call **The Other 4 Percent**. Let me explain this simple concept. Members of the social group "The Other 4 Percent" display and act out antisocial behaviors. There may or may not be laws against their behavior, but it certainly is lacking in moral principles and clearly borders on the illegal. They seem to be totally unbridled by any value system whatsoever. Failing to live a value-driven life poses the risk of being incarcerated in nearly every country on the planet in which any semblance of, or reliance on, the law exists. Men and women who can't act in accordance with behavior responses codified in the laws of that county will be arrested and taken up into whatever the judicial system requires. Most often, those displays of anti-social behaviors lead to jail time, often followed by periods of probation. In the United States, at any given time, about 4 percent of our population is either incarcerated in jail or under the control of a parole officer. Simply put, the other 4 percent are those individuals who display and act out in similar fashion against the laws of the land. They act contrary to positive social values and do harm to others physically, emotionally, or financially. But they have not yet been arrested, gone to court, done jail time, or been on parole. The other 4 percent, at times, morph into the first 4 percent by shooting people from a tower or in a mall; bullying classmates, reporters, and neighbors;

abusing spouses and children; robbing and selling drugs; and undertaking many other infractions of the law. They eventually are caught. They get the jail time and the probation they have surely earned. Regrettably, that pipeline fills with another person who acts irresponsibly and in anti-social ways, so the feeder group of the other 4 percent potentially at least always stays at that number.

My hope with this book is that it might reach some of the other 4 percent, in addition to those who are concerned with bringing up children or adolescent boys into men, or those who are reading this on a simple quest for self-improvement that by doing so, we can reduce the other 4 percent over a generation or two.

Don't become part of the other 4 percent yourself and don't bring up your children that way. If you're an adult and you're part of the 4 percent, if you have reason and will in your repertoire; you can change your life for the better if you want to. Exercise some self-control.

Adopt a set of values such as the ones in this text to govern your behaviors. Set yourself apart from those who hold no values or negative values. Totally separate yourself from those who think being in the other 4 percent category is OK. When I was about three years old, a present was delivered to our house. It was a Christmas gift from one of my aunts and the box was filled with individually wrapped apples. Attractive green tissue fully encased each apple in the box. The apples were layered in an egg carton-like, dappled-mesh cardboard divider, with another layer of apples below it—four layers in all. Because I was at the stage in my life where I could never ask too many questions, I asked my mother why the apples were wrapped in tissue paper. The answer was the first of many times I would hear the cliché, "because one bad apple can spoil the whole bunch." My mother explained that the wrapper would keep the spoilage from one apple from spreading to the whole case of apples. With one apple in twenty-four possibly being bad, the grower-packer was protecting the 96 percent from the 4 percent of bad apples.

Now, much older, I fully appreciate the early life lesson in human relationships, such as in the case of apples where one bad apple can spoil the whole bunch. Experience has taught me that the number comparison is similar as well. About 4 percent of the individuals in any given group of people are spoilers. They spoil the group's productivity, ruin relationships, poison the well with gossip, and they lie, cheat, and complain they are never happy, no matter what. There is nothing that can be done to please them for any length of time. They are selfish and they act entitled. Any bad behavior in the group will be exhibited first within the 4 percent. Unchecked behaviors by this 4 percent group can quickly destroy the sanctity and safety of the entire group they're associating with.

The 4 percent present thinking and speech like this, and they, more regrettably, act like this:

"I am entitled to. . . ."

"The rules don't apply to me."

"The (law, rule, regulation) is stupid, therefore, I can ignore it."

"I know what the rule is, but I don't care. I'm going to break it anyway."

When confronted with their unsocial act, they assault the messenger in ways like the following.

"Who the h*ll do you think you are?"

"Let me be clear with you. If you ever do that to me again, I'll throw you off this f**king balcony!"

"No, no. You're not man enough, you're not man enough. I'll break you in half, like a boy!"

They challenge any attempt to remind them of their infractions with statements like this:

"Go ahead and call the police."

"Who do you think you are? Telling me I have to. . . ."

Some of these examples are from elected officials. They know who they are. You probably do also As an ordinary citizen, It's clear to me that our socialization as men in this country failed when people so lacking in judgment have been elected to the highest offices in the land. Think about this. Out of a population of 317,460,300, only 537 are running this country. And yet we get behaviors that are immoral, unjust, and illegal from some of them. Four percent of this slice of the congressional population is 22.

I have mentioned elected officials for bullying and unethical behavior, however the other 4 percent turns up in all walks of life and all occupations. One of the places they can be most harmful to the innocent is when they turn up on the police forces across our land. Recent examples in New Mexico where officers were overly aggressive in enforcing the law led to the unnecessary death of a homeless man with mental problems. Many other examples exist around the country where the lack of restraint has led to unnecessary death and suffering. The whole Ferguson example still going on began with a lack of respect for authority and a lack of respect by those in authority for some segment of the citizenry there. Two sides of the same coin. Give no respect, get no respect. It's that simple.

We can do better and it starts with an assessment of a man's behavior in relation to the values articulated in this book. Who are the real men in this society deserving of our esteem? What values will define manhood for the rest of this century? A good start begins with those in this text.

What do we do?

The very bottom line: live a value-filled life and don't ever become one of the other 4 percent.

www.ingramcontent.com/pod-product-compliance
Lightning Source LLC
Chambersburg PA
CBHW070534030426
42337CB00016B/2202